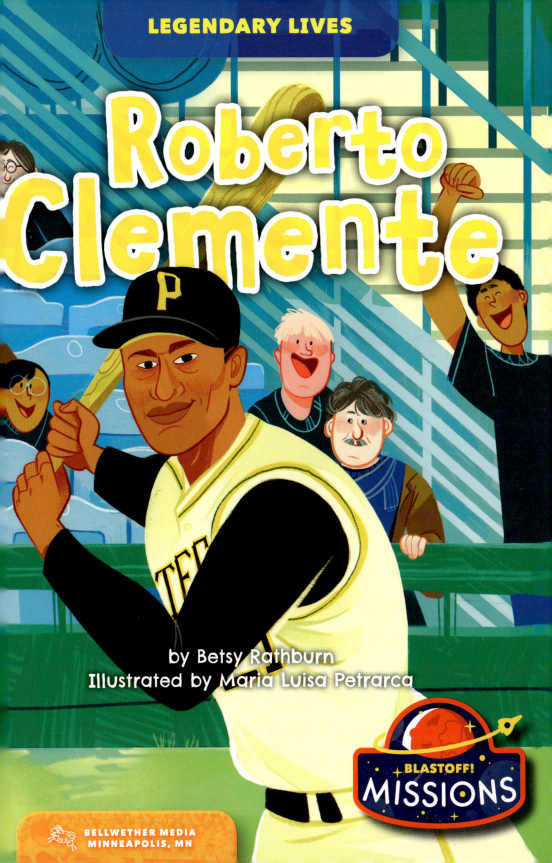

Blastoff! Missions takes you on a learning adventure! Colorful illustrations and exciting narratives highlight cool facts about our world and beyond. Read the mission goals and follow the narrative to gain knowledge, build reading skills, and have fun!

Traditional Nonfiction

Narrative Nonfiction

Blastoff! Universe

MISSION GOALS

> FIND YOUR SIGHT WORDS IN THE BOOK.
> LEARN ABOUT ROBERTO CLEMENTE'S LIFE.
> LEARN ABOUT HOW ROBERTO CLEMENTE HELPED OTHERS.

This edition first published in 2025 by Bellwether Media, Inc.

No part of this publication may be reproduced in whole or in part without written permission of the publisher. For information regarding permission, write to Bellwether Media, Inc., Attention: Permissions Department, 6012 Blue Circle Drive, Minnetonka, MN 55343.

Library of Congress Cataloging-in-Publication Data

Names: Rathburn, Betsy, author. | Petrarca, Maria Luisa, illustrator.
Title: Roberto Clemente / by Betsy Rathburn ; illustrated by Maria Luisa Petrarca.
Description: Minneapolis, MN : Bellwether Media Inc., 2025. | Series: Blastoff! missions. Legendary lives | Includes bibliographical references and index. | Audience: Ages 5-8 | Audience: Grades 2-3 | Summary: "Vibrant illustrations accompany information about the life of Roberto Clemente. The narrative nonfiction text is intended for students in kindergarten through third grade."-- Provided by publisher.
Identifiers: LCCN 2024041933 (print) | LCCN 2024041934 (ebook) | ISBN 9798893042054 (library binding) | ISBN 9798893044003 (paperback) | ISBN 9798893043020 (ebook)
Subjects: LCSH: Clemente, Roberto, 1934-1972--Juvenile literature. | Baseball players--Puerto Rico--Biography--Juvenile literature. | Baseball players--United States--Biography--Juvenile literature.
Classification: LCC GV865 .C45 R37 2025 (print) | LCC GV865 .C45 (ebook) | DDC 796.357092 [B]--dc23/eng/20240912
LC record available at https://lccn.loc.gov/2024041933
LC ebook record available at https://lccn.loc.gov/2024041934

Text copyright © 2025 by Bellwether Media, Inc. BLASTOFF! MISSIONS and associated logos are trademarks and/or registered trademarks of Bellwether Media, Inc.

Editor: Rebecca Sabelko   Designer: Andrea Schneider

Printed in the United States of America, North Mankato, MN.

This is **Blastoff Jimmy**! He is here to help you on your mission and share fun facts along the way!

Table of Contents

Meet Roberto Clemente	4
Starting Out	6
In the Big Leagues	10
A Great Loss	20
Glossary	22
To Learn More	23
Beyond the Mission	24
Index	24

Roberto Clemente's hit soars above the **outfield**. He races around first base. The other team tries to get him out. He is too fast. He slides into second base. Safe!

second base

Starting Out

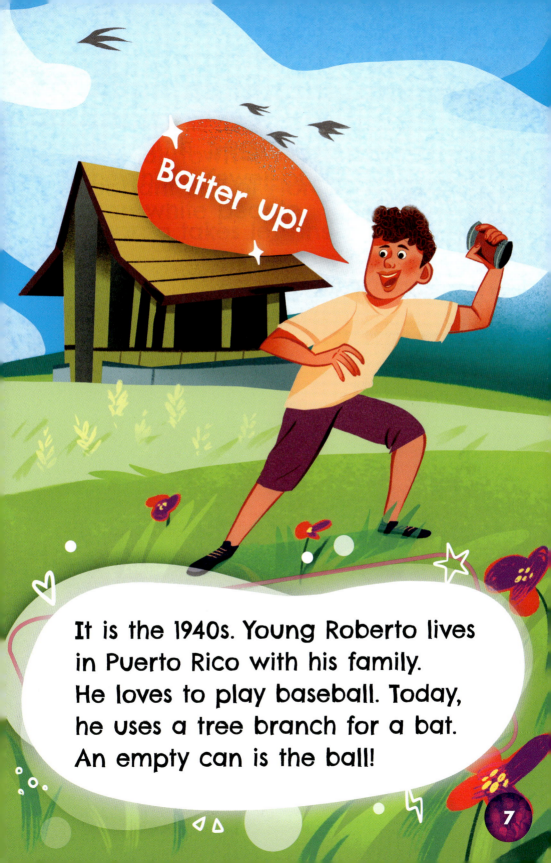

It is the 1940s. Young Roberto lives in Puerto Rico with his family. He loves to play baseball. Today, he uses a tree branch for a bat. An empty can is the ball!

outfield

Scouts notice his strong throwing arm. They see he is a good batter. Roberto soon joins an **amateur** baseball team.

In the Big Leagues

Roberto has been **drafted** by the Pittsburgh Pirates. He is excited to join the team.

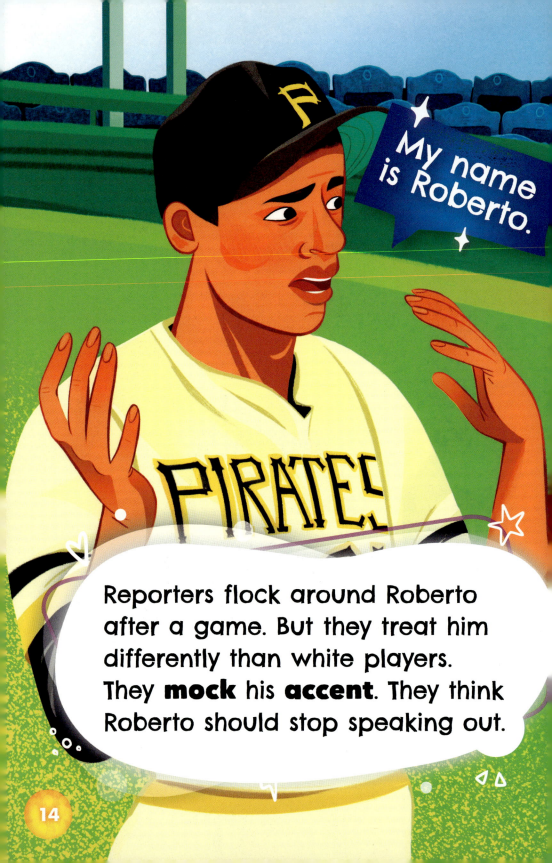

Reporters flock around Roberto after a game. But they treat him differently than white players. They **mock** his **accent**. They think Roberto should stop speaking out.

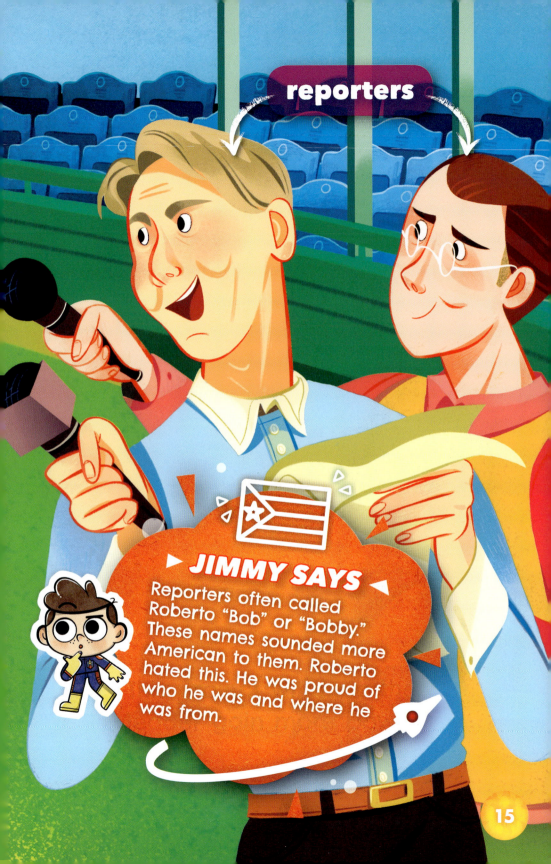

It is the 1971 **World Series**. The Pirates face the Orioles. Roberto steps up to the plate. He swings for the ball. **Home run**! The Pirates go on to win Roberto's second World Series!

> **JIMMY SAYS**
> Roberto won the World Series Most Valuable Player Award in 1971. He was the first Spanish-speaking player to do so!

It is the end of the Pirates' 1972 season. The pitcher winds up. Roberto swings his bat. Hit! Roberto is the first Latin American player to reach 3,000 hits!

A Great Loss

Aaron Judge winning the Roberto Clemente Award

There has been an **earthquake** in Nicaragua. Roberto flies there to help. But his plane crashes. He was one of baseball's greatest players. Today, the Roberto Clemente Award goes to players who commit to helping others.

Roberto Clemente Profile

Born
August 18, 1934, in Carolina, Puerto Rico

Died
December 31, 1972

Accomplishments
Award-winning baseball player who became a role model for Black and Latino players

Timeline

1950: Roberto joins an amateur baseball team

1955: Roberto plays his first game with the Pittsburgh Pirates

1960: Roberto wins his first World Series with the Pirates

1971: Roberto wins his second World Series with the Pirates

1972: Roberto passes away in a plane crash

Glossary

accent–a different way to say a language's words, based on location

amateur–related to a person who does something for pleasure and not for a job

drafted–chosen to play for a team

earthquake–a sudden movement of the earth's crust

home run–a hit where the batter runs all the way around the bases and scores a run; home runs are usually hit over the outfield fence.

league–a group of sports teams that play one another

mock–to make fun of

outfield–the grassy part of a baseball field

racism–unfair treatment of someone based on their race

scouts–people who look for the best players to join their team

segregation–the act of separating people based on their race

World Series–the championship series in Major League Baseball

To Learn More

AT THE LIBRARY

Hanlon, Luke. *Roberto Clemente: Baseball Legend.* Mendota Heights, Minn.: Press Box Books, 2024.

Romo Edelman, Claudia. *Roberto Clemente.* New York, N.Y.: Roaring Brook Press, 2022.

Starr, Abbe L. *Roberto Clemente: Baseball's Biggest Heart.* Minneapolis, Minn.: Lerner Publications, 2023.

ON THE WEB

FACTSURFER

Factsurfer.com gives you a safe, fun way to find more information.

1. Go to www.factsurfer.com.

2. Enter "Roberto Clemente" into the search box and click 🔍.

3. Select your book cover to see a list of related content.

BEYOND THE MISSION

> WHAT FACT FROM THE BOOK DID YOU THINK WAS THE MOST INTERESTING?

> WHAT ELSE WOULD YOU LIKE TO LEARN ABOUT ROBERTO CLEMENTE?

> HOW COULD YOU HELP SOMEONE WHO IS BEING TREATED UNFAIRLY? MAKE A LIST.

Index

accent, 14
amateur, 9
Baltimore Orioles, 17
baseball, 7, 9, 12, 20
drafted, 10
earthquake, 20
hits, 18
Major League Baseball, 12
Most Valuable Player, 17
Nicaragua, 20
outfield, 5, 8, 9
Pittsburgh Pirates, 10, 17, 18
profile, 21
Puerto Rico, 7
racism, 11
reporters, 14, 15
Roberto Clemente Award, 20
scouts, 9
segregation, 11
softball, 8
World Series, 17